THE GREAT BOOK OF ANIMAL KNOWLEDGE

ELEPHANTS

The Largest Land Animals on the Planet

1

Introduction

The largest land mammal in the world is the elephant. Elephants are among the leaders of the jungles and deserts. Their intelligence and strength has been put to use for many years. Sadly, elephants are now endangered, meaning there's only a few left.

What Elephants Look Like

Photo by shankar s. (flickr.com/shankaronline), as licensed under CC BY 2.0 Generic

Elephants have special features including giant ears, tusks, and a really long trunk. They also have thick skin about an inch thick. Their tails are thin strings with bushy tips. The elephant is usually colored gray but some kinds of elephants are dusty brown or reddish brown.

Size and Weight

Photo by Arnaud Boudou (flickr.com/aboudou), as licensed under CC BY-SA 2.0 Generic

Elephants are really large animals. They can grow about 11 feet tall! That's a lot taller than the tallest man in the world, who is only 8 feet. Elephants can also weigh up to 13,000 pounds! That's about half a ships weight.

Senses

Photo by Rod Waddington (flickr.com/rod_waddington), as licensed under CC BY-SA 2.0 Generic

Elephants are near-sighted, meaning they can only see a few inches away; this is because their eyes are small. But their hearing and smelling are very good. Because of their big ears, an elephant is able to hear sounds from very far away.

Teeth

Photo by Gunther Hagleitner (flickr.com/hagleitn), as licensed under CC BY 2.0 Generic

The elephant has 6 to 7 sets of teeth. The elephant's teeth wear away quickly, making way for another set of teeth to grow and move forward to replace the worn out teeth. After the last set has been worn out, the elephant will have no more teeth and they can no longer feed themselves.

Feet

Each of the elephant's foot has 5 toes, but not all of those toes have toe nails. Some elephants just have 3 or 4 nails on their back feet. Did you know that the bone of the elephant's feet is actually standing on tip-toe? Their feet bones are protected by tough, fatty pads for the soles. These pads help support the elephant's feet bones and also help them to walk quietly.

Trunk

Photo by Håkon Thingstad (flickr.com/hakonthingstad), as licensed under CC BY-SA 2.0 Generic

The trunk is probably the most amazing feature of the elephant. You might be surprised to know that there are no bones on the elephant's trunk! This makes the trunk very flexible. The trunk is the one of the most important tools to the elephant; it's used for breathing, smelling, touching, grasping, and producing sound. The tip of the trunk has flaps called fingers; it's used by the elephant to pick up objects.

Tusk

Elephants are born without tusks. Like human teeth, the elephant grows milk tusks and are soon replaced by adult tusks. But there are some elephants that never grow any tusks, like the Asian female elephant. The tusk is used for protection or for battle against other animals. It is also used for digging, stripping bark, and moving things out of the way. The size of the tusk ranges from very long to barely visible.

Where Elephants Live

The grasslands are the elephant's main habitat, but they can also live in savannas, forest areas where there are swamps, or anything in between. Elephants can eat many different plants, so they really can live anywhere with a lot of plants.

What Elephants Eat

Elephants are herbivores, meaning they eat only plants. Elephants eat grass, small plants, bushes, fruits, twigs, tree bark, and roots. The elephant's favorite food is tree bark, which contains calcium and roughage, minerals that help digest the elephant's food. Elephants will also eat soil to get other minerals for their bodies.

What Elephants Do

Photo by shankar s. (flickr.com/ shankaronline), as licensed under CC BY 2.0 Generic

Elephants spend most of their days walking around and eating plants. Elephants are active for 18 to 20 hours a day! While exploring and eating are important to the elephant's day, an elephant also takes time to have fun. They like to play water games with each other or just hang out.

Intelligence

Elephants are some of the most intelligent animals in the world. Their brain is much bigger than any other land animal. Elephants have a very good memory and are very quick learners. They can solve many kinds of problems, like, for example, one elephant was able to use a plastic box by rolling it over and stepping on it to get to a fruit high up on a branch. They can even be taught how to draw and write!

Baby Elephants

Photo by Maureen Didde (flickr.com/maureendidde), as licensed under CC BY 2.0 Generic

A baby elephant is called a calf. Baby elephants stick very close to their mother for a few months. At 4 months old, the calf can start eating some plants, but still needs milk from its mother. Calves can continue drinking their mother's milk for up to 10 years! Baby elephants are very clumsy; they usually always step on their trunks. Calves are born with black or red hair on their foreheads.

Breeding

Photo by Umberto Nicolett (flickr.com/ unicoletti), as licensed under CC BY-SA 2.0 Generic

Elephant breeding is a long cycle. They have long reproductive tracts, long pregnancies, produce calves that involve a long development, and female elephants can only produce one calf every 5 years. The older males, about 40 to 50 years old, are most likely the ones to breed with females. Females can start breeding at the age of 14. It takes about 22 months until a baby elephant is born.

Social Life

While male elephants usually live alone when they're older, female elephants, along with their cubs, form a group, called a herd. The herd is usually led by the most experienced female in that group, called the matriarch. An elephant herd is said to be one of the closest families in the animal kingdom.

Communication

Photo by Christian Haugen (flickr.com/ christianhaugen), as licensed under CC BY 2.0 Generic

Elephants can communicate with each other in many different ways. They usually communicate through rumbling sounds too low for human ears to hear. They're sensitive to vibrations, so elephants can communicate through stamping the ground with their heavy feet. They can also communicate through a trumpet sound, but that's usually when they're about to get attacked. They can communicate together from very far distances.

Predators

Photo by Trish Goebel (flickr.com/106373109@N08), as licensed under CC BY 2.0 Generic

Because of their huge size, adult elephants have no natural predators. But baby elephants are still in danger from predators. Once a baby elephant leaves its mother's side, it is in great danger from lions, crocodiles, and even sometimes hyenas and leopards.

Poachers

The real threat to the elephants are poachers, the people who kill them for their tusks. People make the elephant's tusk into ivory, a hard creamy-white substance used for many different things, like spear tips, bow tips, piano keys, and a whole bunch of other stuff. Because of this, thousands of elephants are killed every year, reducing their numbers dramatically.

Death

Photo by Greg Willis (flickr.com/gregw66), as licensed under CC BY-SA 2.0 Generic

Just like humans, elephants have death ceremonies. Once an elephant dies, its herd members will try to make it alive again by giving it food and water. When they're sure the elephant is really dead, the whole herd will become very quiet and dig a shallow grave for the dead elephant. They will stay near the grave for a few days. Sometimes elephants even go into depression.

Asian Elephants

The Asian elephant is smaller in size than the African elephant. They only have one finger at the tip of their trunk, so instead of being able to pick up objects with their fingers, they have to wrap the object around their trunks. They have small, rounded ears and two humps on top of their heads. Female Asian elephants don't grow a tusk. They can be colored gray, dusty brown, or reddish brown.

African Elephants

Unlike the Asian elephant, the African elephant has two fingers in their trunk, allowing them to pick up objects using their fingers. The African elephant has huge fan ears, covering its whole neck. They have a more rounded head and a single hump at the top of their head.

Get the next book in this series!

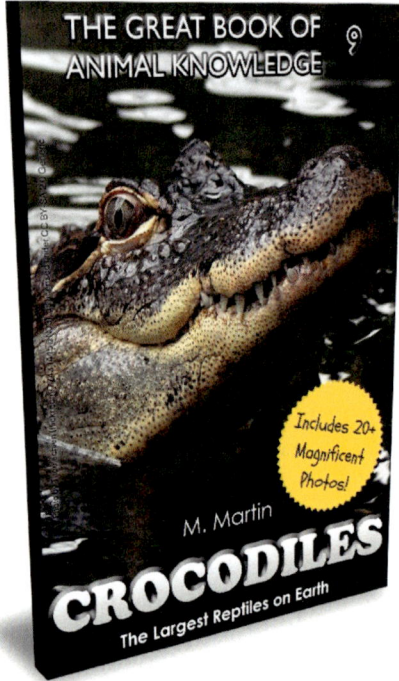

CROCODILES: The Largest Reptiles on Earth

Log on to Facebook.com/GazelleCB for more info

Tip: Use the key-phrase "The Great Book of Animal Knowledge" when searching for books in this series.

For more information about our books, discounts and updates, please Like us on Facebook!

Facebook.com/GazelleCB

Made in the USA
Middletown, DE
26 November 2018